The Classic Collection

·WARM·
AND
WEARABLE

Crochet and Knit

By The Staff of WORKBASKET Magazine

KC PUBLISHING, INC.

700 West 47th Street, Suite 310 • Kansas City, Missouri 64112

·WARM· AND WEARABLE

PROJECT PATTERNS

Classic Mittens
Knit
16

Diamonds in the Rough
Muffler and Mittens
Knit
18

Rose Parade Scarf
and Mitten Set
Knit
22

Twin Snowflake Scarf
and Mitten Set
Knit
27

Cozy Cabled Slippers
Knit
30

Bear Footed Slippers
Knit
32

Panda Slippers
Crochet
34

Slam-Dunk Slippers
Knit
36

High-Top Booties
Crochet
40

Tiny Tyke
Granny Square Ensemble
Crochet
44

Jack and Jill
Sweaters
Crochet
50

Country Tweed Sweater
Crochet
56

Nordic-Style
Pullover Sweater
Knit
62

Reindeer Design
Cardigan
Knit
66

Rippling Waves
Hooded Pullover
Knit
72

USEFUL INFORMATION

Abbreviations & Terms
3

Helpful Hints
4

Reference Guide for
Crocheters
6

Color Photos of Projects
7

Reference Guide for Knitters
15

INTRODUCTION

Contrary to the old adage "cold hands mean a warm heart" — cold hands are usually idle ones. Knitters and crocheters, at least, know how to keep themselves (not to mention family and friends) warm and cozy throughout cold winter months. Scarves, mittens, slippers and sweaters are produced, as if by magic, from the knitting needles and crochet hooks of skilled stitchers. The readers of WORKBASKET Magazine have continually challenged us to provide warm and wearable patterns for their loved ones. In this new Classic Collection book, we've compiled some of the most popular and most often requested patterns from our readers. Whether you begin with a basic, traditional mitten pattern, a pair of whimsical bear slippers or even baby booties designed to resemble high-top sports shoes, you'll be able to make a variety of easy to challenging knit and crochet projects from the patterns included in this book.

In an age where mass-produced apparel is the norm, handmade items take on special significance and value. You'll have a warm sense of pride when the garments you have made yourself receive admiring glances and compliments. Your family also will have that special sense of warmth, knowing the tender-loving care you have stitched into the items made especially for them.

So, don't delay. Begin right now with a project for yourself or someone you love. Cold hands really mean "no mittens" and cold feet will quickly warm up to the idea of knit or crocheted slippers. Warm someone's heart with one of the many warm and wearable projects on the pages that follow.

Kay M. Olson

Executive Editor
WORKBASKET Magazine

ABBREVIATIONS AND TERMS

Crochet

bl	block stitch
CC	Contrasting Color
ch(s)	chain(s)
cl	cluster
dc	double crochet
dec	decrease(s)
dtr	double treble crochet
hdc	half double crochet
inc	increase(s)
lp	loop
MC	Main Color
p	picot
pc	popcorn stitch
rnd(s)	round(s)
sc	single crochet
sk	skip
sl st	slip stitch
sp	space
st(s)	stitch(es)
tr	treble crochet
tr tr	treble treble crochet
yo	yarn over

Knit

CC	Contrasting Color
dec	decrease(s)
inc	increase(s)
K	knit
lp	loop
MC	Main Color
P	purl
psso	pass slip stitch over
rnd(s)	round(s)
sk	skip
sl	slip
sp	space
st(s)	stitch(es)
tbl	through back loop
tog	together
yo	yarn over

Gauge — The number of stitches to the inch horizontally and the number of rows to the inch vertically.

Work Even — Continue working the pattern without increasing or decreasing the row length by adding or omitting any stitches.

HELPFUL HINTS

YARN

Always purchase an extra amount of yarn in the same dye lot. If it is not needed, most shops will give you credit for any unused full balls.

Ply does not determine weight or thickness of yarn. Ply denotes the number of individual yarns twisted together to make a single strand. The thickness depends on the diameter of the yarn — some being very fine, others very bulky.

GAUGE

The most important way to make your project the correct size is to check your gauge. Remember — TO SAVE TIME, TAKE TIME TO CHECK GAUGE. Your own knitting/crocheting tension may require different needle or hook sizes than those given in instructions to achieve the correct stitch gauge.

Hooks and needles recom-mended for different weights of yarns are: baby-weight, D hook and number 3 needles; sport-weight, F-G hook and number 5 needles; worsted-weight, H-J hook and number 8-10 needles; bulky-weight, K hook and number 10-13 nee-dles.

YARN OVERS

Yarn overs can be confusing for both beginning and experienced knitters. Those yarn overs that are most confusing are the ones occurring between knit and purl stitches. To yarn over after a purl stitch, before a knit stitch, move yarn over right-hand needle and knit next stitch in usual manner. To yarn over after a knit stitch, before a purl stitch, move yarn to front (towards you) between the needles, over right-hand needle and back to the front again. Purl the next stitch.

JOINING YARN WHEN KNITTING

When you need to start a new skein of yarn, start a new color or cut out a bad place in the yarn, there are three proven methods of joining. The best way is to drop the end of yarn at the beginning of a row, leaving about a two-inch length, and begin working with the new yarn, leaving about a two-inch length. After the article is finished, thread the yarn ends in a blunt needle and weave them in and out for eight or ten stitches.

You may also join yarn at the end of a row by making a slipknot with the new strand around the previous strand. Draw slipknot close to end of work.

Another method is to work within four inches of end of yarn, then lay a new strand along the old so that about one inch extends beyond last stitch. Knit the four inches with double yarn, cutting the ends after completion of piece.

JOINING YARN WHEN CROCHETING

To start new yarn or a new color, work a stitch up to the last step, pick up the new yarn and complete the last step of the stitch. Keep both loose ends on the wrong side to be woven into the piece later.

CHANGING COLORS WHEN KNITTING

When changing from one color to the next in the middle of a knit row (or anywhere between the two ends, for that matter), twist one color of yarn around the other. The twist should show up on the wrong side of the work. Weave in and trim loose ends later. Neglecting to twist yarn ends around each other at a color change will result in a hole or gap in the work.

Horizontal stripes are easier because color changes are always made at the beginning of a row.

REFERENCE GUIDE FOR CROCHETERS

SINGLE CROCHET

Chain desired number of stitches. Insert hook from front under top two strands of second chain from hook.

Yarn over the hook and draw through stitch (two loops on hook).

Yarn over hook again and draw through two loops (one loop remains on hook) — one single crochet made).

Insert hook under top two strands of yarn on next stitch and repeat previous steps until a single crochet has been made in every stitch of chain; then chain one stitch for turning.

DOUBLE CROCHET

Chain desired number of stitches. Yarn over and insert hook from front under top two strands of fourth chain from hook.

Yarn over again and draw through stitch (three loops on hook).

Yarn over again and draw through first two loops (two loops remain on hook).

Yarn over and draw through two loops (one loop remains) — one double crochet made.

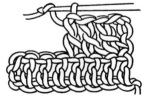

*Yarn over, insert hook in next chain and draw up a loop, yarn over and pull through two loops, yarn over and pull through two loops. Repeat from * until a double crochet has been made in every stitch of chain; then chain three for turning.

Rose Parade and Twin Snowflake Scarf and Mitten Sets
(Knit)

page 22

Diamonds in the Rough Muffler and Mittens
(Knit)

page 18

7

Cozy Cabled Slippers
(Knit)

page 30

Bear Footed Slippers
(Knit)

page 32

Classic Mittens
(Knit)

page 16

Panda Slippers
(Crochet)

page 34

Tiny Tyke Granny Square Ensemble
(Crochet)

page 44

High-Top Booties
(Crochet)

page 40

Jack & Jill Sweaters
(Crochet)

page 50

Slam-Dunk Slippers
(Knit)

page 36

Reindeer
Design
Cardigan
(Knit)

page 66

Nordic-Style
Pullover Sweater
(Knit)

page 62

**Country Tweed
Sweater**
(Crochet)

page 56

Rippling Waves Hooded Pullover
(Knit)

page 72

14

REFERENCE GUIDE FOR KNITTERS

KNITTING A STITCH

Hold needle with cast on stitches in left hand, insert empty needle held in right hand into first stitch on left needle. With yarn at back of work, bring it under and then over right needle point.

Draw newly-formed loop through stitch on left needle.

This newly-formed stitch remains on the right needle. Work into each stitch in the same manner until all stitches have been transferred to the right needle.

PURLING A STITCH

Hold needle with cast on stitches in left hand, insert empty needle from back to front of first stitch on left needle. With yarn at front of work, bring it over and around right needle point.

Draw newly-formed loop through stitch on left needle.

This newly-formed stitch remains on the right needle. Work into each stitch in the same manner until all stitches have been transferred to the right needle.

CLASSIC MITTENS

Materials: Number 4 double pointed needles (dpn); one skein of worsted-weight yarn; stitch markers; and a tapestry needle.

Gauge: 6 sts and 8 rows equal 1 inch

TO SAVE TIME, TAKE TIME TO CHECK GAUGE.

Finished Measurements: From top of fingertips to bottom of cuff, mittens measure 8 (9, 10-1/2) inches. Across the finger portion they measure 2-1/2 (2-7/8, 3-1/4) inches. Directions are given for size small (with medium and large sizes in parentheses).

Cuff: Cast on 32 (34, 36) sts and divide on three dpn. Join and work in K2, P2 ribbing for 3 (3-1/4, 3-1/2) inches. (K2 tog) one (two, two) time(s) in the last rnd — 31 (32, 34) sts. K even for three (four, four) rnds.

Increase Round for Thumb: RND 1 K half of the sts on the next needle, place st marker, inc 1, K1, inc 1, place second st marker, K to end of rnd. RNDS 2-3 K. RND 4 K to and sl marker, inc 1, K to last st before marker, inc 1, sl marker, K to end of rnd. RNDS 5-6 K. Repeat Rnds 4-6 until there are 11 (13, 15) sts between markers, then K two more rnds. K to and sl marker, cast on 2 sts, sl these 2 sts and next 11 (13, 15) sts onto st holder.

Mitten Hand: K around until 1/2 (5/8, 3/4) inch from desired

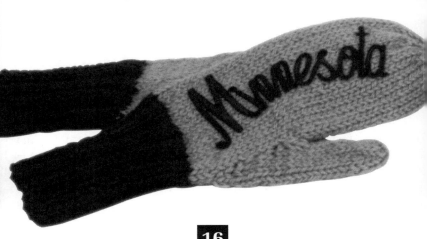

Make mittens for the whole family with this traditional pattern to fit Papa, Mama, Brother, Sister and even baby-sized hands.

length. (K2 tog) two (one, one) time(s) in last rnd — 29 (31, 33) sts. **Decrease RND 1** *K2, K2 tog, repeat from * to last 1 (3, 1) st, K. **RND 2** K. **RND 3** *K2 tog, repeat from * to end of rnd. Cut yarn and thread it through tapestry needle. Pull yarn through and draw up remaining sts.

Thumb: Sl sts from holder and divide onto three needles. K around until thumb measures desired length. **Decrease RND 1** (K2 tog), complete rnd. **RND 2** *K1, K2 tog, repeat from * to end of rnd. **RND 3** K. **RND 4** *K2 tog, repeat from * to end of rnd. Cut yarn and thread it through tapestry needle. Pull yarn through and draw

up remaining sts. Make other mitten the same.

To personalize or make mittens extra special, sew on an appliqué (initials, an animal figure, or the logo of a favorite sports team, for example). Look for appliqués in the sewing notion department; sports team appliqués are available in many sport clothing stores.

DIAMONDS IN THE ROUGH
MUFFLER AND MITTENS

Ruggedly handsome, this muffler and mitten set is bound to be appreciated by the men in your life.

Materials: Approximately 1050 yards sport weight yarn for main color (MC) and 130 yards sport weight yarn for contrasting color (CC); numbers 4 and 6 straight knitting needles; a set of number 4 double pointed needles (dpn); bobbins and holders.

Gauge: With number 6 needles, 6 sts equal 1 inch; 8 rows or rnds equal 1 inch

TO SAVE TIME, TAKE TIME TO CHECK GAUGE.

Right Mitten: With smaller needles and MC, cast on 48 sts. Work in ribbing (K1, P1) for 3-1/2 inches.

Hand: Change to stockinette (K one row, P one row). Beginning with a K row, work first inc for thumb gore. **First Inc Row** K24, inc 1 in next st (first thumb st), K1, inc 1 in next st (last thumb st), K remaining 21 sts. Work three rows even. **Second Inc Row** K24, inc one st in next st, K3, inc one st in next st, K to end of row. Work three rows even. Continue inc one st in first and last thumb st every 4th row, having 2 more sts between incs after each inc row five more times — 17 sts. P one row. **Dividing Row** (Right Side) K24 for back of hand

Shown in color on page 7

☒ CONTRASTING COLOR

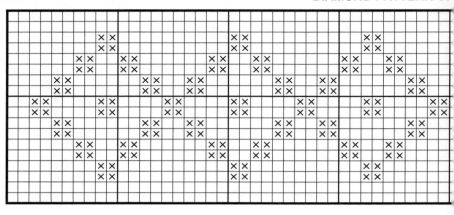

and place on holder; on dpn, K17 thumb sts and cast on 2 sts at end, place remaining 21 sts on holder for palm of mitten. **Thumb:** Divide sts on three dpn; with fourth needle, K around for 2-1/2 inches, dec 2 sts in last rnd. **First Dec** *K1, K2 tog, repeat from * to end of rnd. K one rnd. K2 tog across and fasten off, leaving a yarn end. Draw end tightly through remaining sts and fasten securely. Sl sts for back of hand from holder to a straight needle, join yarn, pick up and K2 sts on cast-on thumb sts, sl palm sts back to needle from holder and K across. Work even in stockinette to 7 inches or desired length above cuff, allowing 1/2 inch for finishing. End with a P row. **First Dec Row** K tog every 3rd and 4th st across row. Work three rows even. **Second Dec Row** K tog every 2nd and 3rd st across row. Work three rows even. **Third Dec Row** K2 tog across row. Finish same as for thumb. Work Diamond Pattern A in duplicate stitch on back of hand. Sew side seam and work in ends.

Left Mitten: Work same as right mitten to first inc row for thumb gore. K21 for palm and work first inc for thumb gore same as right mitten. K24 for back of hand. Work three rows even. Continue working as for right mitten to dividing row, ending with a P row. **Dividing Row** K sts of palm and place on holder, K17 sts for thumb on a dpn and cast on 2 sts. Place sts for back of hand on a holder. Work thumb and complete as for right mitten.

Muffler: With MC and larger needles, cast on 72 sts and work 1-1/2 inches in stockinette (K one row, P one row). Join CC and work

☒ CONTRASTING COLOR

DIAMOND PATTERN B

DUPLICATE STITCH

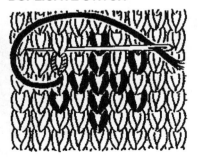

Diamond Pattern B following the chart. Continue with MC until muffler measures 33 inches or until desired length, allowing for about 3 inches to finish. Using CC, work Diamond Pattern B following the chart, then work 1-1/2 inches MC and bind off. Sew sides together making a center seam. Muffler will be double thickness. Fringe each end.

Fringe: Wrap yarn around a 3-inch piece of cardboard and cut one end. Working through both thicknesses of muffler, knot four strands of fringe in every 4th st across each end of muffler. Trim fringe evenly and lightly steam.

Shown in color on page 7

Rose Parade and Twin Snowflake Scarf and Mitten Sets

Rows of roses or double snowflakes adorn warm winter wear to keep adults and kids alike smiling in the snow.

ROSE PARADE ENSEMBLE

Materials: Approximately 1056 yards sport weight yarn for main color (MC) and 130 yards sport weight yarn for contrasting color (CC); numbers 4 and 6 knitting needles; a set of number 4 double pointed needles (dpn); and yarn bobbins.

Gauge: With number 6 needles, 6 sts equal 1 inch; 8 rows or rnds equal 1 inch

TO SAVE TIME, TAKE TIME TO CHECK GAUGE.

Right Mitten — Cuff: With smaller needles and MC, cast on 44 sts. Work in ribbing (K1, P1) for five rows. Change to larger needles and CC, then work 10 rows from chart. With MC and smaller needles, K one row, then work five rows in ribbing — approximately 3 inches for cuff.

Hand — First Inc Row for Thumb Gore: (Right Side) K22, inc one st in next st (first thumb st), K remaining 19 sts. Work three rows even. Start rose pattern from chart.

Second Inc Row K22, inc one st in next st, K3, inc one st in next st, K19 — 48 sts. Continue to inc one st in first and last thumb st every 4th row, having 2 more sts between inc after each inc row four more times. P one row.

Dividing Row (Right Side) K22, place on holder for back of hand, K15 to a dpn for thumb and cast on 2 sts — 17 sts. Sl 19 sts for palm to a holder.

Thumb: Divide sts to 3 dpn and with 4th needle K around for 2 inches. **First Dec Row** *K1, K2 tog, repeat from * around. K one rnd even. **Second Dec Row** K2 tog around. Fasten off, leaving a yarn end. Draw end tightly through all sts and fasten securely. Sl back of hand sts from holder to straight needle, join yarn, pick up and K2 sts of cast-on thumb sts, sl palm sts back to needle from holder and K across.

Work chart until piece measures 6 inches or desired length above cuff, allowing 1/2 inch for finishing, ending with a P row.

First Dec: K tog every 3rd and 4th st across.

Work three rows even. **Second Dec:** K tog every 2nd and 3rd across. Work three rows even. **Third Dec:** K2 tog across. Finish as for thumb. Sew side seam and work in ends.

Left Mitten: Work same as right mitten to First Inc Row for Thumb Gore. K19 for palm and work first inc for thumb gore same as for right mitten. K22 for back of hand. Work three rows

Left Adult Mitten

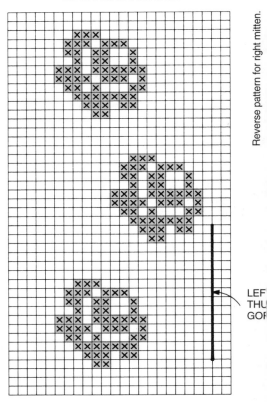

Reverse pattern for right mitten.

LEF
THU
GOI

even. Start rose pattern following chart and work 2nd inc for thumb gore.

Continue to work to correspond to right mitten to Dividing Row, ending with a P row.

Dividing Row K sts of palm and place on holder, K15 for thumb on a dpn and cast on 2 sts. Place sts for back of hand on a holder. Work thumb, then fin-

Adult Scarf

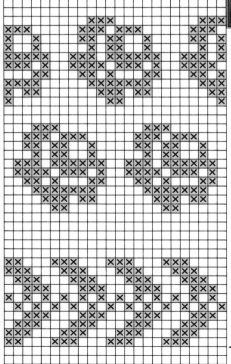

ish mitten to correspond to right mitten.

Scarf: With larger needles and MC, cast on 96 sts. Work in stockinette for 1 inch, join CC and work 36 rows of pattern from chart. Continue with MC for approximately 48 inches or desired length, allowing for approximately 6 inches to finish.

Reverse chart pattern (working upside down) joining CC to work pattern, work 1 inch with MC. Bind off. Sew side together to form

← BEGIN PATTERN

center seam, making scarf a double thickness. Fringe each end.

Fringe: Wrap yarn around a 3-inch piece of cardboard and cut at one end. Working through both thicknesses, knot four strands of fringe in every 4th st across each end of scarf. Trim fringe evenly and lightly steam.

TWIN SNOWFLAKE ENSEMBLE

Materials: Approximately 650 (650, 780) yards main color (MC) and 130 yards contrasting color (CC) sport weight yarn; numbers 4 and 6 knitting needles; a set of number 4 double pointed needles (dpn); and yarn bobbins.

Gauge: With larger needles, 6 sts equal 1 inch; 8 rows or rnds equal 1 inch

TO SAVE TIME, TAKE THE TIME TO CHECK GAUGE.

Finished Sizes: Instructions are given for small size (2-4 years) with medium (5-7 years) and large (8-10 years) in parentheses.

Right Mitten — Cuff: With small needles and MC, cast on 32 (36, 40) sts. Work K1, P1 ribbing for three rows. (**Note:** When changing color in ribbing, K first row before continuing K1, P1.) Change to CC and work three rows ribbing, then alternate two rows each color three times, working six rows MC in last stripe for large only — approximately 2-1/2 (2-1/2, 3) inches ribbing.

Hand: Beginning with a K row, work in stockinette (K one row, P one row) for four rows. Center pattern from chart on sts for back of hand 16 (18, 20) sts. **First Inc Row for Thumb Gore** (Right Side) K16 (18, 20) sts, inc one st in next st (first thumb st), K1, inc one st in next st (last thumb st), K remaining 14 (15,

Left Child Mitten

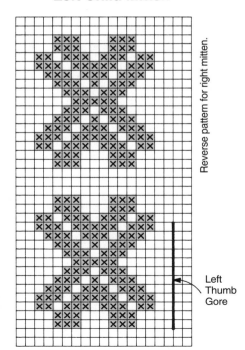

Reverse pattern for right mitten.

Left Thumb Gore

17) sts, P one row. **Second Inc Row** K16 (18, 20) sts, inc one st in next st, K3, inc one st in next st, K to end of row — 37 (40, 44) sts. Continue to inc one st in first and last thumb sts every other row, having 2 sts more between incs after each inc row two (two, three) times. Work three (three, five) rows even, ending with a P row — 41 (44, 50) sts. **Dividing Row** (Right Side) K16(18,20) sts and place on holder for back of hand. K11(11,13) sts to a dpn, cast on 2 sts — thumb sts. K remaining 14 (15, 17) sts and place on holder for palm. Divide thumb sts on three dpn. With 4th needle, K around for 1-1/4 (1-1/2, 1-3/4) inches above cast on sts, dec 1 (1, 0) sts in last rnd. **First Dec Rnd** *K1, K2 tog, repeat from * around. K one rnd even. K2 tog around and fasten off, leaving a yarn end. Draw end tightly through all sts and fasten securely. Sl sts for back of hand from holder to straight needle, join yarn and pick up and K2 sts on cast-on thumb sts, sl palm sts back onto needle and K across. Work, following chart until measurement above cuff is 4 (5, 5-1/2) inches or desired length, allowing 1/2 inch for finishing. End with a P row. **First Dec** K tog every 3rd and 4th st across row. P one row. **Second Dec** K tog every 2nd and 3rd st across row. P one row. **Third Dec** K2 tog across, finish as for thumb. Sew side seam and work in ends.

Left Mitten: Work same as Right Mitten to First Inc Row for Thumb Gore. K14(15,17) sts for palm and work first inc for thumb gore same as right mitten. K16(18,20) sts for back of hand, centering pattern from chart.

Child's Scarf

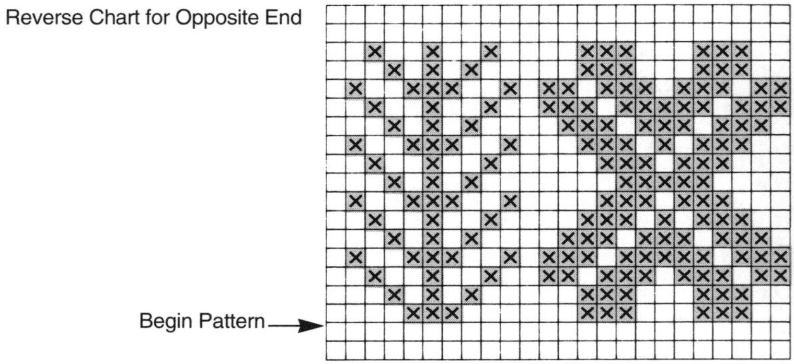

Reverse Chart for Opposite End

Begin Pattern →

Continue to correspond to right mitten to dividing row, ending with a P row. **Dividing Row** K sts of palm and place on holder, K11 sts for thumb on dpn and cast on 2 sts. Place sts for back of hand on a holder. Work thumb and finish to correspond to right mitten.

Scarf: With MC and using larger needles, cast on 72 sts and work 1-1/2 inches in stockinette. With CC, work pattern following chart. Continue with MC until scarf measures 33 inches or desired length, allowing approximately 3 inches to finish. Reverse pattern on chart and work pattern, then work 1-1/2 inches MC in stockinette and bind off. Sew side together to form a center seam, making scarf double thickness. Fringe each end.

Fringe: Wrap yarn around a 3-inch piece of cardboard and cut at one end. Working through both thicknesses, knot four strands of fringe in every 4th st across each end of scarf. Trim fringe evenly and lightly steam.

COZY CABLED SLIPPERS

Materials: 400 yards acrylic worsted weight yarn; 2 yards 5/8-inch ribbon; number 9 knitting needles; a size G crochet hook; and stitch markers.

Gauge: In stockinette, 7 sts equal 2 inches; 5 rows equal 1 inch

TO SAVE TIME, TAKE TIME TO CHECK GAUGE.

Finished Measurements: Directions are given for small/medium (with large in parentheses). Small/medium fits shoes sizes 5-7, and large fits shoe sizes 8-11.

Sole: With two strands of yarn, cast on 46 (50) sts. **ROW 1** P23(25), place marker on needle, P to end of row. **ROW 2** (K1, inc 1 in next st) twice, K to within 4 sts of marker, inc in each of next 8 sts, K to within 4 sts of end, (inc 1 in next st, K1) twice — 58 (62) sts. **ROW 3** P. **ROW 4** (K1, inc one st in next st) twice, K to within 4 (6) sts of marker, inc in each of next 8 (12) sts, K to within 4 sts of

The fun-to-knit cable gives these slippers just enough stretch for a comfortably warm, perfectly pretty fit.

first st again (the one that is now at the end of left-hand needle) and sl both sts from needle; repeat from *, ending K2. **ROW 4** Repeat Row 2. **ROWS 5-8** Repeat Rows 1-4. **ROWS 9-11** Repeat Rows 1-3. **ROW 12** (Wrong Side) Work 18 sts in pattern, *P2 tog, K2 tog; repeat from * seven (nine) times, P2 tog, work remaining 18 sts in pattern. **ROW 13** *K2 tog, yo; repeat from * across, ending K1. **ROW 14** Bind off remaining 53 (57) sts.

Finishing: Sew bottom of sole and back seam. With sole facing and single strand of yarn, work 1 row sc around sole in turning ridge. Fold ribbon in half and draw through yo lps. Tie bow in front. If preferred, make a crocheted cord (pictured) as follows: With double strand, ch 30 inches (about 110 ch). Fasten off, weave in ends. Knot each end and draw through yo holes. Tie bow in front.

end, (inc 1 in next st, K1) twice — 70 (78) sts. **ROW 5** P. **ROWS 6-7** K for turning ridge. Begin pattern.

Pattern: ROW 1 *P2, K2; repeat from *, ending P2. **ROW 2** *K2, P2; repeat from *, ending K2. **ROW 3** *P2, K2 tog (leaving sts on left-hand needle), K

BEAR FOOTED SLIPPERS

*Kids won't have to run around barefoot on cold
floors with these cute bear slippers.*

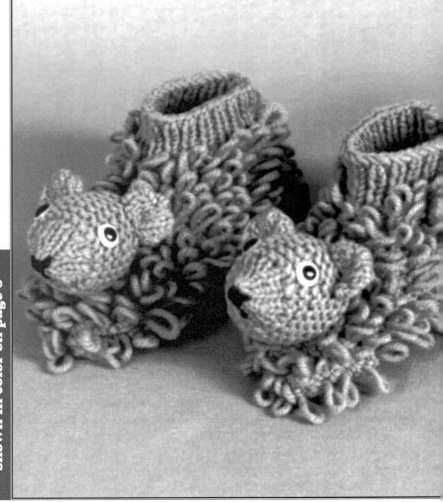

Materials: Approximately 100 (125, 175) yards of worsted weight tan yarn and a few yards of black yarn; number 7 knitting needles; tapestry needle; stitch markers; 12mm crystal animal eyes; and fiberfill.

Gauge: 5 sts and 10 rows equal one inch

TO SAVE TIME, TAKE TIME TO CHECK GAUGE.

Finished Sizes: Instructions are given for size small (with medium and large in parentheses); 4- (6-, 8-) inch foot length.

Special Abbreviation: SSK (Slip, Slip, Knit); Slip 2 sts, K1, pass 2 slipped sts over.

Sole: (Worked in Garter Stitch) Cast on 34 (50, 70) sts. **ROW 1** K16(24,34), place marker, K2, place marker, K16(24,34). **ROW 2** K to one st before marker, inc one st in next st, sl marker, K2, sl marker, inc one st in next st, K to end. Repeat Row 2 until work measures 1 (1-1/4, 1-1/2) inch(es) or until there are 50 (70, 96) sts.

Upper Slipper: ROW 1 K1, *K1, but leave st on left needle, bring yarn forward between needles and wind over left thumb to form lp. Return yarn between needles to back (maintaining lp on thumb) and K the same st again, dropping it off the left needle. Bring yarn forward between the needles and take it over the right needle to make a yo, pass the 2 sts just worked over this yo and off the right needle, K next st*; repeat from * to * across. **ROWS 2 and 4** K to 2 sts before marker, K2 tog, sl marker, K2, sl marker, SSK, K to end. **ROW 3** K2, repeat from * to * as in Row 1 until 2 sts before marker, SSK, sl marker, K2, K2 tog, repeat from * to * as in Row 1 to end of row. Repeat Rows 1-4 until 32 (36, 44) sts remain. Work two rows even. Work K1, P1 ribbing for 1 inch. Bind off loosely.

Head: Cast on 6 sts. **ROW 1** K across. **ROW 2** K, inc one st in every st — 12 sts. **ROW 3** Repeat Row 2 — 24 sts. **ROWS 4-20** K across. **ROW 21** K2 tog across — 12 sts. **ROW 22** P. **ROW 23** *K2, K1; repeat from * across — 8 sts. **ROW 24** P. **ROW 25** K. Cut yarn, thread needle and draw yarn through open sts. Sew side seams.

Ears: Cast on 7 sts. **ROWS 1, 3, 5, 7 and 9** P. **ROW 2** K2 tog, K3, K2 tog — 5 sts. **ROW 4** K2 tog, K1, K2 tog — 3 sts. **ROW 6** Inc one st, K1, inc one st — 5 sts. **ROW 8** Inc one st, K3, inc one st — 7 sts.

Sew ears' side seams; attach ears and eyes to head. Embroider nose. Stuff head. Sew cast-on edge seam. Attach one head to slipper. Sew slipper seams.

PANDA SLIPPERS

Shown in color on page 9

Identical panda pals will keep little toes warm and cozy.

Materials: Approximately 240 yards ecru and 240 yards black acrylic worsted weight yarn; a size G crochet hook; and a tapestry needle.

Gauge: 4 sc equal 1 inch

TO SAVE TIME, TAKE TIME TO CHECK GAUGE.

Finished Sizes: Instructions are given for children's sizes 11-12 (about a 5-year-old), 13-1 (about a 6-year-old), 2-3 (about a 7- or 8-year-old).

Heel Tab: With ecru, ch 6. Sc in 2nd ch from hook and each ch across — 5 sc. Ch 1, turn. Working in *back loops only*, sc in next st and each st across. Ch 1, turn. Repeat this row four (five, six) more times. *Do not fasten off.*

Main Section: Work 9 (11, 13) sc on side of tab, 5 sc on lower edge, 10 (12, 14) sc on other side of tab — 25 (29, 33) sc. Ch 1, turn. **NEXT ROW** Working in *back lps only*, sc in next st and each st across. Ch 1, turn. Repeat this row until 6 (7, 8) inches from start of Main Section. *Do not ch 1*. Turn.

Toe Shaping: Working in *back lps only*, sc in next st, *sc 2 tog, repeat from * across row — 14 (16, 18) sts. Ch 1, turn. Repeat this row — 7 (8, 9) sts. **NEXT ROW** Sc in 0 (1, 0) st, *sc 2 tog, repeat from * across row — 4 (5, 5) sts. *Do not fasten off.*

Join Instep: Fold Main Section in half lengthwise. Working in sl st, join from toe up to 4-1/2 (5, 5-1/2) inches, leaving remainder free for foot opening. Then continue row of sl st around foot opening. Fasten off.

Eyes: With ecru, ch 3. **ROW 1** 2 sc in 2nd ch from hook, 2 sc in remaining ch. *Do not turn.* **ROW 2** With black, ch 1. Work 3 sc at end of row, work 2 sc on underside of first row, work 3 sc at end of row, work 2 sc on top side of first row, sl st to first sc. **ROW 3** Ch 1, sc in first st, 3 sc in next st, sc in next 4 sc, 3 sc in next sc, sc in next 3 sc, sl st to sc at beginning. Fasten off.

Nose: With black, ch 3. Close ring with sl st to first ch. Ch 1, work 6 sc in ring, ending with sl st to first sc. Fasten off.

Ears: With black, ch 6. **ROW 1** Beginning in 2nd ch from hook, work 5 sc across. Ch 1, turn. **ROW 2** Sc across. Ch 1, turn. **ROW 3** Work 2 sc tog, sc in next sc, 2 sc tog. Ch 1, turn. **ROW 4** Work 3 sc tog. Fasten off.

Finishing: Sew eyes on each side of center seam right below foot opening. Sew ears 1/4 inch above eyes. Sew nose on center seam about 3/4 inch below eyes. With single strand of black and tapestry needle, work mouth details in straight stitch.

Shown in color on page 11

Slam-Dunk Slippers

These high-top booties are cute and practical. They're toddler-tested and mother-approved.

Materials: Approximately 250 yards white, 250 yards red and 250 yards blue acrylic sport weight yarn; number 5 knitting needles; and a pair of 18-inch dress shoe laces for sizes 1 and 2 or a pair of 24-inch dress shoe laces for sizes 3, 4 and 5.

Gauge: In stockinette, 11 sts and 16 rows equal 2 inches; in garter stitch, 11 sts and 24 rows equal 2 inches

TO SAVE TIME, TAKE TIME TO CHECK GAUGE.

Finished Measurements:

Length of Sole: 3-1/2 (4, 4-1/2, 5, 5-1/2) inches

Width of Sole: 2 (2, 2-1/4, 2-1/4, 2-1/4) inches

Height at Back of Ankle: 2-3/4 (2-3/4, 3-1/2, 3-1/2, 3-1/2) inches

The booties are sized corresponding to actual shoe sizes and fastened with regular shoe laces. Directions are given for shoe size 1 (0-3 months) with sizes 2 (3-6 months), 3 (6-9 months), 4 (9-12 months) and 5 (12-15 months) in parentheses.

Special Abbreviation: SKP (Slip, Knit, Passover). This decrease is worked as follows: Slip one st (K-wise) from the left-hand to the right-hand needle. K next st. Passover by taking the tip of the left-hand needle and lifting the slipped st up and over the knitted st and off the end of the right-hand needle.

Lower Body of Bootie: With blue, cast on 50 (56, 62, 66, 72) sts marking the center 6 sts of cast-on row. Working in garter stitch, K four rows. With white, K two rows. Cut white, leaving a 3-inch tail. With blue, K three rows.

Divide for Top of Toe/Tongue: (Wrong Side) With blue yarn, K14(15,17,18,19), sl the sts just knitted (found on right-hand needle) to stitch holder, bind off 8 (10, 11, 12, 14) sts, K6, sl the 6 sts found on right-hand needle to stitch holder, bind off 8 (10, 11, 12, 14) sts, K14(15,17,18,19). Cut blue, leaving a 6-inch tail for seaming. With wrong side facing you and beginning at outer edge, sl the first 14 (15, 17, 18, 19) sts onto end of knitting needle — 28

(30, 34, 36, 38) sts.

Ankle: ROW 1 (Right Side) With white and outside of bootie facing you, K across row joining sides of ankle. **ROW 2** (Wrong Side) Cast on 2 sts at end of needle. Beginning with 2 sts just cast on, K3, P26(28,32,34,36), K1 — 30 (32, 36, 38, 40) sts. **ROW 3** Cast on 2 sts at end of needle. Beginning with cast-on sts, K across all sts — 32 (34, 38, 40, 42) sts. **ROWS 4, 6, 8, 10, 12, 14 and 16** K3, P until 3 sts remain, K3. **ROW 5** (Eyelet and Dec Row) K2 tog, yo, K1, SKP K8(9,11,12,13), K2 tog, K2, SKP K8(9,11,12,13), K2 tog, K1, yo, K2 tog — 28 (30, 34, 36, 38) sts. **ROW 7** K across. **ROW 9** (Eyelet and Dec Row) K2 tog, yo, K1, SKP, K6(7,9,10,11), K2 tog, K2, SKP, K6(7,9,10,11), K2 tog, K1, yo, K2 tog — 24 (26, 30, 32, 34) sts. **ROW 11** K across. **ROW 13** (Eyelet and Dec Row) K2 tog, yo, K1, SKP, K until 5 sts remain, K2 tog, K1, yo, K2 tog — 22 (24, 28, 30, 32) sts. **Note:** For sizes 1 and 2 only, skip rows 14-17 and work border. **ROW 15 (Sizes 3, 4 and 5 only)** K across. **ROW 17** Repeat Row 13 — 26 (28, 30) sts. Work border.

Border: K three rows even. Bind off all sts (K-wise). Fasten off.

Upper Toe: Sl the 6 sts from stitch holder onto needle. With red, work in stockinette stitch inc one st each side *every other row* two (two, three, three, three) times — 10 (10, 12, 12, 12) sts. Work even until upper toe measures 1-1/2 (1-3/4, 2, 2, 2-1/4) inches from joining, ending with a K row.

Tongue: ROW 1 K2, P6(6,8,8,8), K2. **ROW 2** K across. Repeat Rows 1-2 for 1-3/4 (1-3/4, 2-1/4, 2-1/4, 2-1/4) inches from first row of tongue, ending with Row 2. K three rows in garter stitch and then bind off (K-wise).

Sole: With red and right side of toe facing you, pick up 6 sts using the back lps of the sts marked on cast-on row. K across row. Working in garter stitch, join sole to lower body at end of each row as you work (see Joining Sole to Lower Body), inc one st *each side next and every other row* two (two, three, three, three) times — 10 (10, 12, 12, 12) sts. Work even for 30 (36, 38, 42, 44) rows — 34 (40, 44, 48,

50) rows total. Dec one st each side *next and every other row* two (two, three, three, three) times. Bind off (K-wise).

Joining Sole to Lower Body: You may join sole to lower body by sewing it to lower body after it is knitted or in the following manner as you work: *At the end of each row*, pick up a st in next closest inside lp of cast-on row onto right-hand needle with other sts of sole. At the beginning of next row, K2 tog (st picked up and first st of sole).

Finishing: Sew center back seam of lower body of booties joining edges of garter stitch rows. Graft bound-off edge of sole to lower body at back of heel or join sole to lower body if not joined as you knit. Sew upper toe to bound-off edges of lower body. Weave in ends. Thread shoe lace through yo eyelets on slanted edges. Hand stitch purchased star-shaped appliqués, if desired. Repeat directions for remaining bootie.

HIGH-TOP BOOTIES

Just like the knit version but especially designed for crocheters, these high-top slippers are cute as well as practical.

Materials: Approximately 200 yards white, 200 yards blue and 200 yards red acrylic sport weight yarn; a size F crochet hook; and a pair of 18-inch shoe laces.

Gauge: 5 sc and 5 rows equal 1 inch

TO SAVE TIME, TAKE TIME TO CHECK GAUGE.

Finished Measurements:

Length of Sole: 3-1/2 (4, 4-1/2, 5) inches

Width of Sole: 2 (2, 2-1/2, 2-1/2) inches

Height at Back of Ankle: 2-3/4 (2-3/4, 3-1/2, 3-1/2) inches

The booties are sized corresponding to actual shoe sizes and fastened with regular shoe laces. Instructions are given for shoe size 1 (0-3 months) with sizes 2 (3-6 months), 3 (6-9 months) and 4 (9-12 months) in parentheses.

Note: Unless specified, always work sts through both lps of sc and dc. Sole is worked in rnds. Do not turn work at end of each rnd.

Sole: With blue, ch 11 (13, 14, 16). **RND 1** 3 Sc in 2nd ch from hook, sc in each of next 8

Shown in color on page 10

(10, 11, 13) chs, 3 sc in last ch. *Do not turn.* Continue sc in each of next 8 (10, 11, 13) sts on opposite side of ch, join with sl st to beginning of rnd — 22 (26, 28, 32) sc. **RND 2** Ch 1, *2 sc in each of next 3 sc, sc in each of next 8 (10, 11, 13) sc; repeat from * once, join — 28 (32, 34, 38) sc. **RND 3** Ch 1, *(2 sc in next sc, 1 sc in next sc) three times, sc in each of next 8 (10, 11, 13) sc; repeat from * once, join — 34 (38, 40, 44) sc. **RND 4** Ch 1, *(2 sc in next sc, sc in each of next 2 sc) three times, sc in each of next 8 (10, 11, 13) sc; repeat from * once, join — 40 (44, 46, 50) sc. **RND 5 (Sizes 3 and 4 only)** Ch 1, *(2 sc in next sc, sc in each of next 3 sc) three times, sc in each of next 0 (0, 11, 13) sc; repeat from * once, join — 40 (44, 52, 56) sc. **All Sizes:** Sc in each sc around, join — 40 (44, 52, 56) sc. Do not fasten off.

Lower Body of Foot: This part is worked in joined rows instead of rnds so that the pattern will look the same when working bootie ankle. Ch 3, turn. **ROW 1** With inside of sole facing you and working in *front lps only,* dc in 2nd sc from hook and in every sc around. Join white with sl st to top of ch-3 — 40 (44, 52, 56) dc (ch 3 counts as 1 dc). Ch 1, turn. **ROW 2** With white, sc in every dc, ending with last sc worked in top of ch-3 — 40 (44, 52, 56) sc.

Join blue. Ch 3, turn. **ROW 3** With blue yarn, dc in 2nd sc from hook and in each sc, join — 40 (44, 52, 56) dc. Fasten off. Mark the 4th (4th, 5th, 5th) dc to left of joining.

Ankle: ROW 1 With outside of bootie facing you, join white yarn in marked st. Ch 1, sc in next 20 (20, 25, 25) sc, beginning in st where yarn is joined — 20 (24, 27, 31) sts remain for toe of bootie. Ch 3, turn. **ROW 2** Dc in 3rd sc from hook, dc in each of next 16 (16, 21, 21) sc, sk 1 sc, dc in remaining sc — 18 (18, 23, 23) dc. Ch 1, turn. **ROW 3** Sc in each of next 5 (5, 7, 7) dc, sk 1 dc, sc in each of next 6 (6, 7, 7) dc, sk 1 dc, sc in each of next 5 (5, 7, 7) dc, ending with last sc worked in top of ch-3 — 16 (16, 21, 21) sc. Ch 3, turn. **ROW 4** Dc in 3rd sc from hook, dc in each of next 12 (12, 17, 17) sc, sk 1 sc, dc in remaining sc — 14 (14, 19, 19) dc. **ROW 5 (Sizes 3 and 4 only)** Ch 1, turn. Sc in each st across row, ending with last sc worked in top of ch-3 — 19 sc. **ROW 6 (Sizes 3 and 4 only)** Ch 3, turn. Dc in 3rd sc from hook, dc in each of next 15 dc, sk 1 dc, dc in remaining sc — 17 dc. **All Sizes:** With inside of bootie facing you, work 7 (7, 10, 10) sc across slanted ankle edge, working 2 sc in each dc row and 1 sc in each sc row, ending with 1 sc in st where yarn was joined to crochet ankle. Fasten off.

Other Slanted Edge: With inside of bootie facing you, join yarn in st where last of Row 1 of ankle was worked. Ch 1, work 7 (7, 10, 10) sc across slanted ankle edge, placing 1 sc in st where yarn was joined, and working 1 sc in each sc row and 2 sc in each dc row. Join with sl st to top of ch-3 of last row of ankle. Fasten off.

Upper Toe and Tongue: With red, ch 14 (16, 18, 20). **ROW 1** (Right Side) Beginning in 2nd ch from hook, sc in each of next 12 (14, 16, 18) ch, 3 sc in last ch. *Do not turn.* Continue sc in each of next 12 (14, 16, 18) sc on opposite side of ch — 27 (31, 35, 39) sc. Ch 3, turn. **ROW 2** Beginning in 2nd sc from hook, dc in each of next 11 (13, 15, 17) dc, 3 dc in each of next 3 sc, dc in each of next 12 (14, 16, 18) sc; ch 1, turn. **ROW 3** Sc in each of the next 12 (14, 16, 18) dc, *2 sc in each of next 1 (1, 2, 2) dc, sc in each of next 2 (2, 1, 1) dc; repeat from * twice, sc in each of next 10 (12, 13, 14) dc, working last sc in top of ch-3. Mark 8th (8th, 10th, 10th) st from each corner on long sides of tongue. Work 6 sc along straight short edge of tongue, join with sl st to first sc of row. Fasten off.

Joining Upper Toe and Tongue to Lower Body of Bootie: Place pieces wrong sides together, matching upper toe portion of tongue and lower body of bootie. With outside of bootie facing you, join red at bottom of left slanted edge. Sc *back loop* of lower body and *front loop* of upper toe between markers — 20 (24, 27, 31) sc.

Upper Edging and Eyelets: With red and starting at bottom of slanted edge, work 1 (1, 2, 2) hdc, *ch 1, sk 1 sc, 1 hdc; repeat from * two (two, three, three) times. Work 2 sc in top corner, sc across top of bootie, 2 sc in other top corner, 1 hdc in first sc of slanted edge, *ch 1, sk 1 sc, 1 hdc; repeat from * two (two, three, three) times, work 1 (1, 2, 2) hdc, join with sl st to first sc worked when joining upper toe to lower body, turn. Sl st in sts on slanted edge. Ch 1, turn. With outside of bootie facing you and working from left to right, work a row of reverse sc across top of ankle, turn. Sl st in sts along other slanted edge. Fasten off.

Sole Edging: With red and bottom of sole facing away from you, join yarn in the back lp of a sc in the heel portion of bootie. Ch 1, sc in the back lps around bottom of bootie, join with sl st. Fasten off. Weave in ends. Make second bootie same as first. Thread lace through eyelets. Hand stitch purchased star-shaped appliqués, if desired.

TINY TYKE GRANNY SQUARE ENSEMBLE

Grandma's favorite little one will stay warm in this granny square sweater. Add a stylish tam and coverlet to complete this sweet set that's perfect for traveling to Grandma's house.

Materials: For the sweater and tam, approximately 560 yards pastel variegated (MC), 185 yards pastel blue and 185 yards pastel pink acrylic sport weight yarn; sizes F and G crochet hooks; and five 3/4-inch buttons. For the coverlet only, approximately 370 yards pastel variegated (MC), 370 yards pastel pink and 370 yards pastel blue acrylic sport weight yarn; a size G crochet hook.

Gauge: 4-1/2 hdc equal 1 inch; 3-1/2 rows equal 1 inch; granny squares measure 2-1/2 inches

TO SAVE TIME, TAKE TIME TO CHECK GAUGE.

Finished Sizes: Sweater and Tam is Toddler size 1. Coverlet measures approximately 25 x 25 inches.

SWEATER

Granny Squares: With F hook and pink, ch 4. Join with sl st to first ch to form ring. **RND 1** Ch 3, 2 dc in ring, ch 1, *3 dc in ring, ch 1, repeat from * twice. Join with sl st in top of ch-3 at beginning of rnd. Fasten off. **RND 2** Join MC in any ch-1 sp. Ch

Shown in color on page 10

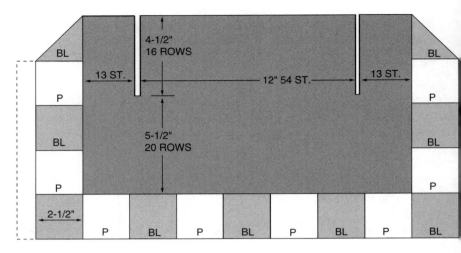

3, 2 dc in same sp, ch 1, 3 dc in same sp, ch 1, *(3 dc, ch 1, 3 dc) in next ch-1 sp, ch 1, repeat from * twice, sl st in top of ch-3 at beginning of rnd. Fasten off. **RND 3** Join blue in any ch-1 sp along side of square, ch 3, 2 dc in same sp, ch 1, *(3 dc, ch 1, 3 dc) in corner ch-1 sp, ch 1, 3 dc in next ch-1 sp, ch 1, repeat from * three times. Sl st in top of ch-3. Fasten off.

Half Granny: With pink, ch 3, join to form ring. **ROW 1** Ch 3, (2 dc, ch 1, 3 dc) in ring. Join MC, turn. **ROW 2** Ch 3, 2 dc in first dc, ch 1, (3 dc, ch 1, 3 dc) in ch-1 sp of Row 1, ch 1, 3 dc in ch-3 of Row 1, turn. **ROW 3** Join blue, ch 3, 2 dc in first dc, ch 1, 3 dc in next ch-1 sp, ch 1, (3 dc, ch 1, 3 dc) in next ch-1 sp, ch 1, 3 dc in next ch-1 sp, ch 1, 3 dc in top of ch-3. Fasten off.

Sweater Body: Make seven granny squares with pink centers and blue borders; eight squares with blue centers and pink borders. Sew nine squares in a strip, alternating colors with blue-bordered squares at beginning and end for lower edge of sweater. Join MC in first st of 2nd square from right end. Ch 2. Working in *front lps only*, work 80 hdc across seven squares, leaving first and last squares free. Ch 2, turn. **Next Row** Work hdc in each st across. Ch 2, turn. Continue to work even until 5-1/2 inches from beginning of hdc pattern, ending on right side.

Shape Armholes: (Right Front) Work across 13 hdc. Ch 2, turn. Work even until 4-1/2 inches above beginning of armhole shaping. Fasten off.

Back: Join MC in last st of right front, ch 2, work in hdc across 54 sts. Ch 2, turn. Work even in hdc until back is same as front. Fasten off.

Left Front: Join MC in last st of back, ch 2, work hdc across 54 sts. Ch 2, turn. Finish to correspond to right front. Sew together three granny squares and a half granny square for neck shaping for each front, alternating colors. Sew to loose square on each side of front and to front of sweater.

Sleeves: (Make two) Make three granny squares: two with blue borders and one with pink border. Sew together in a panel alternating colors. With MC and working in *back lps only*, work 33 hdc across one length of panel. Ch 2, turn. Continue working in hdc, inc one st each side every other row six times — 45 hdc. Work even until piece measures 8 inches. Fasten off.

Cuff: Join blue to beginning edge of granny square panel. Work two rows sc. Join pink, work three rows sc. Join blue, work two rows sc. Fasten off.

Finishing: Sew shoulder and sleeve seams. Sew in sleeves. Join blue at lower edge of left front. Work one row sc across lower edge, 46 sc up right front, sc around neck edge, 46 sc down left front. Join to first sc of rnd. Do not fasten off yarn. Ch 1, turn.

Note: For a boy's sweater, the following instructions should be reversed — button band is on right side, buttonhole band is on left.

Left Button Band: With blue, work one row sc in each sc of left front — 46 sc. Join pink, work three rows sc. Join blue, work two rows sc. Now, in the last row, work 2 sc in corner st, 4 sc across bottom of button band, join in first sc of lower edge. Fasten off.

Right Buttonhole Band: Join blue at neck edge and work 46 sc down right front. Join pink, work one row sc. Ch 1, turn.

Making Buttonholes: ROW 1 Sc, *ch 3, sk 3 sc, 7 sc, repeat from * three times, ch 3, sk 3, 2 sc. Ch 1, turn. **ROW 2** Sc in each sc and ch across. Join blue. Ch 1, turn. Work one row sc. Fasten off. Turn work and join yarn in last st of lower edge border. **Next Row** Work 4 sc across lower edge of band, 2 sc in corner st, sc in each st up right front, 2 sc in corner st, 4 sc across top of band. Continue around neck edge working in *back lps only* of each sc, 4 sc across top of button band, join yarn in first st. Fasten off.

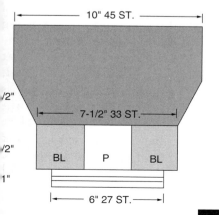

10" 45 ST.

7-1/2" 33 ST.

/2"

/2"

1"

BL   P   BL

6" 27 ST.

TAM

Crown: With pink and G hook, ch 4. Join with sl st to first ch to form ring. **RND 1** Ch 3, 2 dc in ring, ch 1, *3 dc in ring, ch 1, repeat from * four times, join with sl st in ch-3. Fasten off pink. Join MC in any ch-1 sp. **RND 2** Ch 3, (2 dc, ch 1, 3 dc) in same sp, *(3 dc, ch 1, 3 dc) in next ch-1 sp, ch 1, repeat from * four times, join with sl st in ch-3. Fasten off. Join blue in any ch-1 sp. **RND 3** Ch 3, (2 dc, ch 1, 3 dc) in same sp, ch 1, *(3 dc, ch 1, 3 dc) in next ch-1 sp, ch 1, repeat from * four times, join in ch-3. Join MC in any ch-1 sp in center of a cluster. **RND 4** Ch 3, (2 dc, ch 1, 3 dc) in same sp, ch 1, (2 dc, ch 1, 2 dc) in ch-1 sp between clusters, ch 1, *(3 dc, ch 1, 3 dc) in center of cluster, ch 1, (2 dc, ch 1, 2 dc) between clusters, ch 1, repeat from * four times, join in ch-3. **RND 5** Sl st to ch-1 sp in center of cluster, ch 3, (2 dc, ch 1, 3 dc) in same sp, ch 1, (2 dc in next sp, ch 1) three times, *3 dc, ch 1, 3 dc in center of next cluster, ch 1, (2 dc in next sp, ch 1) three times, repeat from * four times, join in ch-3. Fasten off.

Side Motifs: (Make six — three with pink centers and three with blue centers.) Work as for granny squares in sweater for three rnds. **RND 4** Join MC in any ch-1 sp after a corner group, ch 3, 2 dc in same sp, ch 1, *3 dc in next ch-1 sp, ch 1, (3 dc, ch 1, 3 dc) in corner sp, ch 1, 3 dc in next ch-1 sp, ch 1, repeat from * twice, ending last repeat with corner clusters, ch 1, join to ch-3 at beginning of rnd.

Ribbed Band: With MC and F hook, ch 7. **ROW 1** Sc in 2nd ch from hook and in each ch across — 6 sc. Ch 1, turn. **ROW 2** Sc in back of first 5 sc, through both lps of 6th sc. Ch 1, turn. Repeat Row 2 until band measures 17 inches when slightly stretched. Fasten off.

Finishing: With wrong sides together and using sl st, crochet one side of granny square to one side of crown. Join other squares to the other five sides alternating colors. Join sides of squares in same manner. Join ends of band together and sew to cap with lower edge of tam slightly overlapping band.

blue, pink, MC.

Finishing: Sew three squares together alternating colors, sew to one side of Central Square. Sew four squares together, then sew to 2nd side of square alternating colors. Sew four squares together and join to 3rd side; sew five squares together and join to 4th side.

Border: Join blue in any ch-1 sp. Work in granny pattern for two rnds. Fasten off. Join pink, work one rnd. Fasten off. Join blue, work two rnds. Work one rnd sc around entire edge. Fasten off.

COVERLET

Central Square: With blue, ch 4. Join in first ch to form ring. **RND 1** Ch 3, 2 dc in ring, ch 1, *3 dc in ring, ch 1, repeat from * twice, join with sl st in top of ch-3, sl st to next ch-1 sp. Ch 3.

Continue as for granny square in sweater using the following color sequence: Rnds 1-3: blue; Rnds 4-6: MC; Rnds 7-8: pink; Rnd 9: blue; Rnds 10-11: pink; Rnds 12-13: MC; Rnds 14-15: blue; Rnd 16: pink; Rnds 17-18: blue. Fasten off.

Smaller Squares: Work as for first six rnds of Central Square in the following sequence: make eight squares of two rnds each pink, blue, MC; eight squares of two rnds each

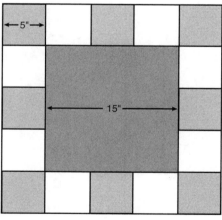

Note: Block squares to measure before sewing together. Block again before beginning border.

Shown in color on page 11

JACK AND JILL SWEATERS

A v-neck pullover for him and a similarly-styled cardigan for her are perfect for rough-and-tumble play.

JILL'S CARDIGAN

Materials: 750 (750, 100) yards variegated (MC) and 250 yards yellow (CC) baby/fingering weight yarn; a size G crochet hook; and four 1/2-inch buttons.

Gauge: 11 sts equal 2 inches; 5 rows equal 1 inch.

TO SAVE TIME, TAKE TIME TO CHECK GAUGE.

Finished Measurements: Toddler size 1 (21 inches across chest); Toddler size 2 (22-1/2 inches across chest); Toddler size 3 (24 inches across chest). Directions are given for T1 (with T2 and T3 instructions in parentheses).

Special Abbreviation: phdc (post half double crochet). Yo, insert hook from front to back in front around post of first hdc, yo, draw lp around post to front of work, yo, draw through 3 lps on hook.

Back Ribbing: With CC, ch 14. **ROW 1** Hdc in underside of 3rd ch from hook and in each ch to end — 12 hdc. Ch 2, turn. **ROW 2** Yo, insert hook from front to back in front around post of first hdc, yo, draw lp around post to front of work, yo, draw through 3 lps on hook (phdc made), *yo, insert hook from front to back around post of next hdc, yo, draw lp through, yo, draw through 3 lps on hook (phdc made). Repeat from * to end. Ch 2, turn. Repeat Row 2 until there are 28 (30, 32) ch-2 lps along each row edge. Draw MC through lp on hook. *Do not turn.*

Back Body — Foundation Row: Working in ch-2 lps along row edge with right side of ribbing facing, work 3 sc in first ch-2 lp, 2 sc in each ch-2 lp to within last ch-2 lp, 3 sc in last ch-2 lp — 58 (62, 66) sc. Ch 1, turn. **ROW 1** Sc in first sc, dc in next sc, *sc in next sc, dc in next sc, repeat from * ending hdc in last sc. Ch 1, turn. **ROW 2** Sc in hdc, dc in sc, *sc in dc, dc in sc, repeat from * ending hdc in last sc. Ch 1, turn. Repeat Row 2 for pattern until piece measures 7-1/2 (8, 8-1/2) inches.

Raglan Armhole: Sl st in first 4 sts, work pattern to last 4 sts. Ch 1, turn. Draw up lp in each of next 2 sts, yo, draw through 3 lps on hook (one st dec), work pattern to last 2 sts, dec one st. Continue to dec one st each end every other row six (seven, 10) times, then every row until 18 (20, 22) sts remain. Fasten off.

Right Front Ribbing: Work same as Back Ribbing, until there are 27 (29, 31) ch-2 lps along row edge. **Note:** When pattern stitch ends with sc, and there is no dec at beginning of next row, ch 2, turn.

Right Front Body — Foundation Row: With MC, work 2 sc in each ch-2 lp to last ch-2 lp, 3 sc in last ch-2 lp (seam edge) — 55 (59, 63) sts. **ROW 1** Work pattern across ending sc in last st. Ch 1, turn. **ROW 2** Dec one st (front edge), dc in next st, work pattern to end. Ch 1, turn. **ROW 3** Work pattern to last 2 sts, dec one st. Ch 1, turn. Repeat Rows 2-3 12 (13, 14) times, then keeping established pattern, dec one st at front edge *every other row* seven (eight, nine) times, and *at same time*, when piece measures same as back to arm-

hole, beginning at seam edge, shape armhole same as back. Dec last 2 sts. Fasten off.

Left Front: Work same as Right Front reversing all shaping.

Sleeve Ribbing: With CC, ch 12. Hdc in 3rd ch from hook and in all chs to end — 10 hdc. Work ribbing as on back until there are 13 (14, 15) ch-2 lps along row edge. Change to MC. *Do not turn.*

Foundation Row: Work 4 (4, 3) sc in first ch-2 lp, *2 sc in next ch-2 lp, 3 sc in next ch-2 lp, repeat from * to end. Work pattern on 34 (36, 38) sts for 1 inch, inc at beginning and end of next row (see note on Right Front), and repeat inc every inch three more times. Work pattern on 42 (44, 46) sts until sleeve measures 7-1/2 (8, 8-1/2) inches.

Raglan Cap: ROW 1 Sl st over 4 sts, work pattern to last 4 sts. Ch 1, turn. **ROW 2** Work pattern across. **ROW 3** Work pattern, dec at beginning and end of row. Repeat Rows 2-3 six (seven, nine) more times, then repeat Row 3 until 4 sts remain. Fasten off.

Finishing: Sew raglan caps to front and back raglan armholes. Sew sleeve and side seams. With right side facing, holding CC on wrong side of work, work one row sl st, spacing sts to keep edge flat, along shaped edge of both fronts (do not work along edge of ribbing). **ROW 1** With CC, work sl sts along front edge, work one row sc, sc in each st along sleeve edge, sk every 4th st, sc along back neck edge, sc along sleeve edge, sc in each sl st. *Do not turn.* **ROW 2** Ch 1, working from left to right, insert hook in next sc, draw up lp, yo, draw through 2 lps on hook (reverse sc made), work reverse sc in each sc. Fasten off.

Finishing: Sew two buttons at free edge of waist ribbing and two buttons at seam edge of ribbing.

JACK'S V-NECK SWEATER

Materials: Fingering/baby weight yarn in the following amounts and colors: approximately 500 (750, 750) yards pastel green (MC) and 250 (250, 500) yards pastel variegated (CC); and a size G crochet hook or size needed to obtain gauge.

Gauge: 11 dc equal 2 inches; 4 rows (2 sc and 2 dc) equal 1 inch

TO SAVE TIME, TAKE TIME TO CHECK GAUGE.

Finished Measurements: Toddler size 1 (21 inches across chest); Toddler size 2 (22 inches across chest); Toddler size 3 (23 inches across chest). Directions are given for T1 (with T2 and T3 in parentheses).

Special Abbreviation: phdc (post half double crochet). Yo, insert hook from front to back in front around post of first hdc, yo, draw lp around post to front of work, yo, draw through 3 lps on hook.

Back Ribbing: With MC, ch 14. **ROW 1** Hdc in underside of 2nd ch from hook and in each ch to end — 12 hdc. Ch 2 (counts as first ch-2 lp), turn. **ROW 2** Yo, insert hook from front to back in front around post of first hdc, yo, draw lp around post to front of work, yo, draw through 3 lps on hook (phdc made), *yo, insert hook from front

to back around post of next hdc, yo, draw lp through, yo, draw through 3 lps on hook (phdc made). Repeat from * to end. Ch 2, turn. Repeat Row 2 until there are 28 (30, 32) ch-2 lps along each row edge. Fasten off. Turn ribbing so that first ch-2 lp is at beginning of work. **Note:** To change colors, draw new color through last 2 lps of st on hook.

Back Body — Foundation Row: Join CC in first ch-2 lp, ch 1. Working in ch-2 lps along row edge with wrong side of ribbing facing, work 2 sc in first (2nd, 3rd) ch-2 lps. With MC, work 2 sc in each ch-2 lp to last ch-2 lp, 3 sc in last ch-2 lp — there are 2 (4, 6) CC sc, 55 (57, 60) MC sc. Ch 2, turn (ch-2 does not count as a st). **ROW 1** With MC, *work 4 (2, 4) dc, yo, insert hook from front to back in front around post of next sc, (yo, draw through 2 lps on hook) twice (phdc made). Repeat from * 12 (13, 14) more times, then work 3 (1, 0) dc. With CC, dc in each of last 2 sc. Ch 1, turn. **ROW 2** Sc in 3 (5, 7) sts. With MC, sc in each dc and phdc to end. Ch 2, turn. **ROW 3** *Dc in next 3 sc, yo, insert hook around post of phdc, draw lp through (yo, draw through 2 lps on hook) twice phdc, repeat from * to last 4 (6, 8) sc. With CC, dc in each sc. Ch 1, turn. Keeping in established pattern work one more CC st *every* row 19 (17, 15) more times, every other row five (seven, nine) times — 22 (25, 28) CC sts. Piece should measure approximately 7-1/2 (8, 8-1/2) inches. **Note:** To dec sc, draw up lp in each of next 2 sts, yo, draw through 3 lps on hook. To dec dc, yo, draw up lp, yo in next st, yo, draw through 2 lps on hook, yo, draw through 3 lps on hook.

Raglan Armholes: Sl st over 4 sts, work pattern to last 4 sts. Ch 1, turn. Dec one st at beginning and end of next row, repeat dec *every other row* five (six, seven) times, continue armhole dec every row, working one more CC st *every other row* until 17 (19, 21) sts remain. There should be one MC st. Fasten off.

Front Body: Work same as Back Body, reversing color pattern until there are 3 armhole dec — 22 (24, 26) MC sts and 21 (23, 25) CC sts. MC st is center st.

V-Neck: Continue armhole dec, work to center st, turn. Dec one st at neck edge every other row five (six, seven) times. Continue raglan until one st remains. Fasten off. Sk center st. Work other side to correspond, reversing all shaping.

Sleeves: With CC, ch 12. Work ribbing as on back, on 10 hdc, until there are 13 (14, 15) ch-2 lps. Fasten off.

Foundation Row: Join yarn in first ch-2 lp, work 4 (4, 3) sc in first ch-2 lp, *2 sc in next ch-2 lp, 3 sc in next ch-2 lp. Repeat from * to last ch-2 lp, work 4 (3, 4) sc in last lps — 33 (36, 39) sc. **ROW 1** Work 2 (1, 2) dc, *phdc, work 3 sts, repeat from * ending 2 (1, 2) dc. Ch 2, turn. **ROW 2** Sc in each dc and phdc. Ch 1, turn. Work pattern for 1 inch, inc one st each end, repeating inc every inch three more times. Work pattern on 43 (45, 47) sts until piece measures 7-1/2 (8, 8-1/2) inches. Ch 1, turn.

Raglan Cap: Sl sts over 4 sts, ch 1, work pattern to last 4 sts. Ch 2, turn. Dec one st at beginning and end of next row, repeating dec *every other row* three (seven, seven) times, then dec *every row* until 5 sts remain. Fasten off.

Finishing: Sew raglan caps to front and back armholes. Matching colors, beginning at center back neck, work one row sc around entire neck edge. Join with sl st. *Do not turn.* Working from left to right, *insert hook in first sc behind hook, draw lp through, yo, draw through 2 lps on hook. Repeat from * around. Join with a sl st. Fasten off.

COUNTRY TWEED PULLOVER

Any little boy or girl will fall in love with this roomy, warm and stylish pullover sweater just right for brisk, autumn weather.

Materials: Approximately 540 (540, 670) yards "tweed" color (A) and 800 (940, 1070) yards solid color (B) sport weight yarn; and sizes D and G crochet hooks.

Gauge: Three squares equal 2 x 2 inches **TO SAVE TIME, TAKE TIME TO CHECK GAUGE.**

Finished Measurements: size 4 (30 inches across chest); size 6 (33 inches across chest); size 8 (36 inches across chest). Directions are given for size 4 (with size 6 and size 8 in parentheses).

Special Abbreviation: trcl (treble crochet cluster). *Yo twice, insert hook in next st, yo and draw yarn through st, yo and draw through 2 lps twice, ending with 2 lps on hook. Repeat from * in same st, ending with 3 lps on hook. Yo and draw through last 3 lps.

Pattern Stitch: ROW 1 (Wrong Side) Sk first ch-2, tr in next sc, *ch 2, sk next ch-2, tr in next sc. Repeat from * number of times indicated in instructions, ch 1, turn. **ROW 2** (Right Side) Sc in first tr, *working behind

Shown in color on page 13

57

square, 2 trcl over ch-2 at base of square, sc in next tr, repeat from * number of times indicated in instructions, work last sc in 3rd ch of ch-6, ch 6, turn. Alternate Rows 1 and 2 for pattern (these two rows equal one row of squares).

Waistband: With D hook and A, ch 15. **ROW 1** Sc in 2nd ch from hook and in each ch across — 14 sc. Ch 1, turn. **ROW 2** Sc in back lp of each sc across — 14 sc. Ch 1, turn. Repeat Row 2 until waistband ribbing measures 11 inches when slightly stretched, ending ch 1. Change to G hook, work 70 (76, 82) sc evenly across long edge of ribbing. Ch 6, turn.

Back Body: ROW 1 (Wrong Side) Sk first 3 sc, tr in 4th sc, *ch 2, sk 2 sc, tr in 3rd sc, repeat from * 21 (23, 25) times — 23 (25, 27) squares worked across. Ch 1, turn. **ROW 2** *Sc in top of tr, working behind square, sk sc under tr and work trcl in each of 2 sc at base of square. Repeat from * 22 (24, 26) times, ending with sc in 3rd ch of ch-6. Ch 6, turn. Alternate Pattern Stitch rows seven (eight, nine) times over 23 (25, 27) squares, ending on an even row. Ch 1, turn.

Chest Band: ROW 1 With A, sc in each sc, 2 sc over each ch-2. Fasten off, join B when working off 2 lps of last sc. Ch 1, turn. **ROW 2** Sc in each sc across. Ch 6, turn. **ROW 3** With

B, work Row 1 of Back Body. **Note:** To change colors for checkered pattern, with sc in top of tr, bring new color across back of work, twist new color around old, work off last 2 lps of sc with new color, drop old color. **ROW 4** With B, sc in top of tr, *work trcl in each sc at base of square, sc in next tr, change to A. Work 1 trcl in each of the 2 sc at base of square, sc in next tr, change to B. Repeat from * across alternating colors B, A, B, A, etc. Change to A in last sc, fasten off B at end of row. With A, ch 6, turn. **ROW 5** With A, work Row 1 of Pattern Stitch. **ROW 6** Work Row 2 of Pattern Stitch, alternating colors A, B, A, B, etc. **ROW 7** With B work Row 1 of Pattern Stitch. **ROW 8** Work Row 2 of Pattern Stitch, alternating colors B, A, B, A, etc. *Do not change to A with last sc.* With B, ch 1, turn. **ROWS 9-10** With B, repeat Rows 1-2 of Chest Band (sc rows).

Left Sleeve: End Row 10 with ch 47 (50, 53), remove hook from lp, but do not fasten off.

Right Sleeve: Join another ball of B, ch 42 (45, 48). With right side facing, join ch to first sc of Row 10. Fasten off this ball of yarn.

Sleeves and Top of Sweater: ROW 1 With wrong side facing, insert hook back into last ch of ch-47(50, 53), tr in 9th ch from

hook, *ch 2, sk next 2 ch, tr in next ch, repeat from * 12 (13, 14) times, working last tr in first sc of body. Ch 2, sk 2 sc and with next tr in next sc, continue Row 1 of Back Body across. Repeat from * across foundation ch of right sleeve, ending ch 1, turn — 14 (15, 16) squares made for each sleeve and 23 (25, 27) squares across body. **ROW 2** *Sc in top of tr, work trcl in each of 2 ch at base of square, repeat from * 13 (15, 16) times, continue Row 1 of Back Body across. Repeat from * across foundation ch of left sleeve, alternating Pattern Stitch rows seven (eight, nine) times over 51 (55, 59) squares, ending on an even row. Ch 6, turn.

Left Neck Shaping: ROW 1 Work Row 1 of Pattern Stitch over first 20 (21, 22) squares, ch 3, sl st in next sc (1 dec), turn. **ROW 2** To fill in dec: *Yo, working from back of dec, insert hook over ch-2 at base of dec, yo and draw yarn up, yo and draw through 2 lps, repeat from * in same st, ending with 3 lps on hook. Yo and draw through last 3 lps (1 dcl made). Work trcl over same ch-2, with sc in next tr, continue Row 2 of Pattern Stitch to end. Ch 6, turn. **ROW 3** Repeat Row 3 of Pattern Stitch over 19 (20, 21) squares, work dec over last square, turn. **ROW 4** Repeat Row 2. Fasten off at end of row.

Right Neck Shaping: ROW 1 With wrong side facing, join B to 9th sc from left shoulder shaping, ch 3. With tr in next sc, continue Row 1 of Pattern Stitch over remaining 20 (21, 22) squares — 1 dec made at beginning of this row. Ch 1, turn. **ROW 2** Work Row 2 of Pattern Stitch to dec. To fill in dec: Work 1 trcl and 1 dcl over ch-2 at base of dec, sl st in sc where B is joined, turn. **ROW 3** Work 2 sc over ch-3 and sc in top of tr, ch 3, with tr in next sc, continue Row 1 of Pattern Stitch to end of row. Ch 1, turn. **ROW 4** Repeat Row 2 of Pattern Stitch, working sl st in sc at top of first tr of previous row. Fasten off.

Front Body: Work as for Back Body. Repeat Rows 1-3 of Chest Band, but in Rows 4 and 8, join A with sc at top of first tr and alternate A, B, A, B, etc., working off last sc with A. In Row 6, join B with sc at top of first tr, alternate colors B, A, B, A, etc., working off last sc lps with B. From Row 9 of Chest Band, continue working as for Back Body until 14 (16, 18) rows of sleeves have been completed. **Note:** Front right sleeve instructions are as for back left sleeve; front left sleeve as back right sleeve.)

Right Neck Shaping: ROW 1 Work Row 2 of Pattern Stitch over first 21 (22, 23) squares, ch

3, sl st in next sc — 1 dec, turn. **ROW 2** Fill in dec as for Back Left Neck Shaping, continue Row 2 of Pattern Stitch to end of row. **ROW 3** Repeat Row 1 of Right Neck Shaping, working dec over last square before dec of previous row, turn. **ROW 4** Repeat Row 2 of Right Neck Shaping. **ROWS 5-6** Repeat Rows 3-4 of Right Neck Shaping. Fasten off.

Left Neck Shaping: ROW 1 With wrong side facing, join B to 8th sc from Right Neck Shaping, ch 3. With tr in next sc, continue Row 2 of Pattern Stitch to end of row — 1 dec made at beginning of this row. **ROW 2** Work Row 2 of Pattern Stitch to dec, fill in dec as for Right Back Neck Shaping, turn. **ROW 3** Work 2 sc over ch-3 and sc in top of tr, ch 3. With tr in next sc, continue Row 3 of Pattern Stitch to end of row. Ch 1, turn. **ROW 4** Repeat Row 2 of Right Neck Shaping. **ROWS 5-6** Repeat Rows 3-4 of Left Neck Shaping. Fasten off.

Finishing: Join front to back at shoulders, sides and underarms.

Neck Band: With A and size D hook, ch 7. **ROW 1** Sc in 2nd ch from hook and in each ch across — 6 sc. Ch 1, turn. **ROW 2** Sc in back lp of each sc across — 6 sc. Ch 1, turn. Repeat Row 2 until neck band fits around neck edge of sweater when slightly stretched. Fasten off. Sew neck band in place around neck edge.

Cuff: (Make two) With A and size D hook, ch 11. **ROW 1** Sc in 2nd ch from hook and in each ch across — 10 sc. Ch 1, turn. **ROW 2** Sc in back lp of each sc across — 10 sc. Ch 1, turn. Repeat Row 2 until cuff measures 6 inches when slightly stretched. Sew to end of sleeve, stretching cuff and easing sleeve to fit. (It will be necessary to ease sleeve considerably.) Sew other cuff and sleeve. For blocking, follow directions given on yarn label.

NORDIC-STYLE PULLOVER SWEATER

Styled after the famous Norwegian ski sweaters, this child-size pullover is great to wear whether or not there's snow on the ground — or if your kids prefer wheels to blades on their skates.

Materials: Approximately 480 (480, 720) yards Main Color (MC) and 240 yards Contrasting Color (CC) acrylic sport weight yarn; numbers 6 and 8 knitting needles; a number 6 circular needle; and three stitch holders.

Gauge: 9 sts equal 2 inches; 10 rows equal 2 inches

Finished Measurements: size 6 (29-3/4 inches across chest); size 8 (31-1/2 inches across chest); size 10 (33-1/2 inches across chest). Directions are given for size 6 (with size 8 and size 10 in parentheses).

TO SAVE TIME, TAKE TIME TO CHECK GAUGE.

Note: When changing colors,

Shown in color on page 12

be sure to twist yarn on wrong side from underneath to prevent holes.

Back: With small needles and MC, cast on 67 (71, 75) sts. Work in ribbing (K1, P1) for 2 (2-1/2, 3) inches, ending on right side and inc one st at beginning and end of row — 69 (73, 77) sts. Change to larger needles and P one row. Working in stockinette (K right-side rows, P wrong-side rows) follow Chart 1 working Rows 1-26 then Rows 1-12. Following Chart 2, repeat Rows 1-6 until back measures 16 (17, 18) inches from beginning, ending on wrong side. With MC bind off 23 (24, 25) sts, work center 23 (25, 27) sts and place on holder, bind off remaining sts.

Front: Work same as Back for 14 (15, 16) inches from beginning, ending on wrong side.

Neck Shaping: Work 29 (30, 31) sts, place on holder for left shoulder. With MC work center 11 (13, 15) sts, place on holder for center front, work remaining sts. Working each side sepa-

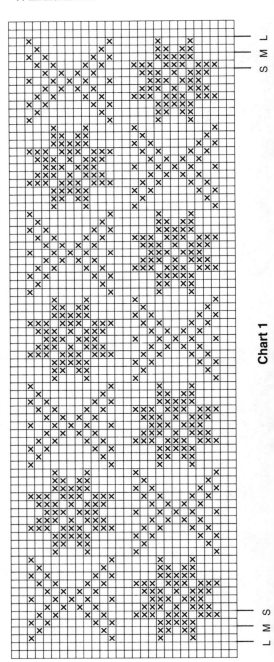

Chart 1

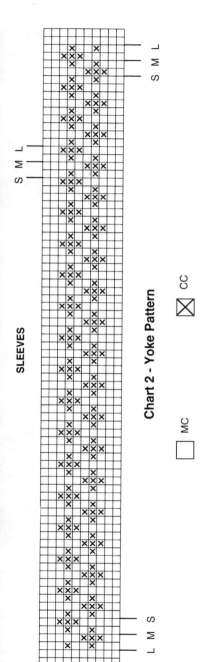

Chart 2 - Yoke Pattern

CC ⊠

MC □

rately, bind off 3 sts once at neck edge, then 2 sts once, and one st once — 23 (24, 25) sts. Work even until front measures same as back to shoulder. Bind off remaining sts. Reversing shaping, work other side to correspond.

Sleeves: With smaller needles and MC, cast on 27 (29, 31) sts. Work in ribbing for 2 (2-1/2, 3) inches, ending on right side. Change to larger needles, P one row, inc 14 (16, 18) sts evenly spaced — 41 (45, 49) sts. Work even for 4 inches from beginning. Following pattern in Chart 2, inc one st every six rows nine times — 59 (63, 67) sts. When sleeve measures 14-1/2 (15-3/4, 17) inches from beginning, bind off loosely in MC.

Finishing: Sew Front to Back at shoulders. With circular needle and MC, right side facing, pick up and K58(62,66) sts around neck edge. Work in rnds of ribbing (K1, P1) for 1 inch. Bind off in ribbing. Mark Front and Back at side edges 6-1/2 (7, 7-1/2) inches down from shoulder seam for sleeve placement. Sew sleeves between markers. Sew side and sleeve seams.

Shown in color on page 12

REINDEER DESIGN CARDIGAN

The reindeer design is duplicate stitched on this classic cardigan, so you can make one with the reindeer for Christmas and one without for any other time of the year.

Materials: A 3-ply sport weight yarn in the following amounts and colors: approximately 700 (700, 950, 1260) yards white (A), 235 yards red (B) and 235 yards green (C); numbers 5 and 7 knitting needles; six 1/2-inch buttons; stitch holders; and a tapestry needle.

Gauge: In stockinette with number 7 needles, 5 sts equal 1 inch; 7 rows equal 1 inch

DUPLICATE STITCH

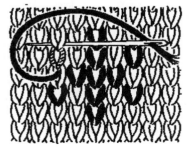

☐ WHITE   ☒ GREEN   ⦿ RED

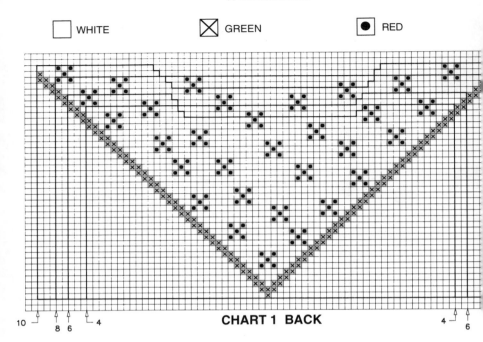

CHART 1 BACK

TO SAVE TIME, TAKE TIME TO CHECK GAUGE.

Note: Directions are given for size 4 (with sizes 6, 8 and 10 in parentheses).

Back: With C and smaller needles, cast on 51 (56, 59, 63) sts. Work in K1, P1 ribbing for 1-1/2 inches, ending right side. **Next Row** (Wrong Side) P, inc 9 (9, 11, 12) sts evenly spaced across row — 60 (65, 70, 75) sts. With A and larger needles, continue in stockinette (K one row, P one row) until

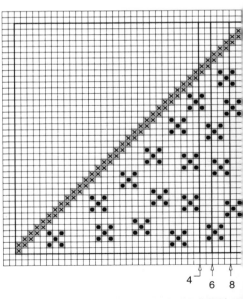

CHART 2 LOWER FRONT

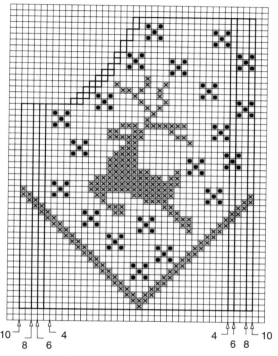

CHART 3 UPPER FRONT

piece measures 14-3/4 (15-3/4, 16-3/4, 17-3/4) inches from beginning.

Neck Shaping: Next Row Work 16 (18, 19, 20) sts, join another strand of yarn, bind off center 28 (29, 32, 35) sts, complete row. Working *both sides at same time*, dec one st each neck edge on next row. Bind off remaining 15 (17, 18, 19) sts *each side*. Beginning at one upper side edge, work duplicate stitch pat-

tern from Chart 1.

Left Front: With C and smaller needles, cast on 30 (32, 35, 38) sts. Work in ribbing until 1-1/2 inches from beginning, ending right side. **Next Row** (Wrong Side) P, inc 5 sts evenly spaced over first 25 (27, 30, 33) sts, sl last 5 sts to a holder — 30 (32, 35, 38) sts. With A and larger needles, continue in stockinette until piece measures 13 (14, 15, 16) inches from beginning, ending right side.

Neck Shaping: Next Row (Wrong Side) Bind off 6 (6, 7, 8) sts, complete row. Dec one st at neck edge every row five (five, seven, nine) times, every other row four (four, three, two) times. Bind off remaining 15 (17, 18, 19) sts. Beginning at lower center front edge, work duplicate stitch pattern from Chart 2. Beginning at upper edge, find center stitch and work pattern from Chart 3.

Right Front: Work same as Left Front for three rows. **Next Row** (Buttonhole) Rib 2 sts, yo, work 2 sts tog, rib across — buttonhole made. Complete same as Left Front reversing shaping and pattern from chart.

Sleeves: With C and smaller needles, cast on 30 (30, 32, 34) sts. Work in ribbing for 1 inch, ending right side. **Next Row** (Wrong Side) P, inc 5 sts evenly spaced — 35 (35, 37, 39) sts. With A and larger needles, work in stockinette, inc one st each edge every 6th row 10 (11, 12, 13) times — 55 (57, 61, 65) sts. Work even until piece measures 10-1/2 (11-1/2, 12-1/2, 13-1/2) inches from beginning. Bind off. Beginning at center st above ribbing, work duplicate stitch pattern from Chart 4.

Finishing — Left Placket: Sl 5 sts from holder to smaller needles. With C, continue in ribbing

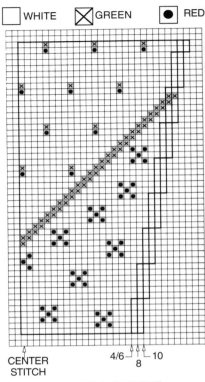

WHITE   ⊠ GREEN   ● RED

CENTER STITCH   4/6   8   10

CHART 4 SLEEVE

until slightly stretched placket measures length of front to beginning of neck shaping. Sl sts to a holder. Stitch placket to cardigan edge. Mark front for four more buttons evenly spaced between first buttonhole and 1-1/2 inches below neck shaping.

Right Placket: With C and smaller needles, work five placket stitches from holder in ribbing as established. Work buttonholes as follows at each marker: rib 2, yo, rib 2 tog, rib 1. When placket measures to neck edge, sl sts to a holder. Stitch placket to cardigan edge.

Neck Band: Sew shoulder seams. From right side, with smaller needles and C, pick up 5 sts from right placket holder and work in ribbing as established, pick up sts evenly spaced along neck edge to left placket holder, work 5 placket sts in ribbing. Work three rows ribbing. On following row, work buttonhole same as placket. When band measures 1 inch, bind off in ribbing. Mark each side 5-1/2 (5-3/4, 6, 6-1/2) inches below shoulder seam. Sew in sleeves between markers. Sew side and sleeve seams. Sew on buttons.

Shown in color on page 14

RIPPLING WAVES HOODED PULLOVER

The interesting pattern stitch of this warm, hooded sweater creates a deep, rich texture. Plus, it's plenty roomy and sized extra long for a comfortable, flattering fit.

Materials: 1800 yards bulky weight yarn; numbers 8, 9 and 10 knitting needles; and a 16-inch number 8 circular needle.

Gauge: In Pattern Stitch, 13 sts equal 4 inches; 30 rows equal 4 inches. In stockinette with number 9 needles, 14 sts equal 4 inches; 19 rows equal 4 inches

TO SAVE TIME, TAKE TIME TO CHECK GAUGE.

Finished Measurements: 44-1/2 inches across bust and 28 inches long.

Special Abbreviation: PBL (Pick up Back Loop). Pick up back lp of st five rows below next st and K tog with next st.

Back: With number 10 needles, cast on 72 sts, K two rows.

Change to number 8 needles.

Drawstring Channel: Increase Row (Wrong Side) P and inc one st in every st across row — 144 sts. Thread a CC yarn through every other st and hold at back of work. Working on front sts only, work four rows stockinette stitch (K one row, P one row), ending on wrong side. Thread a CC yarn through these sts and place back sts on needle. From wrong side of work, work four rows stockinette (both P sides face one another on inside of channel). Sl other needle through sts at front of work. Sl sts at back of work to any smaller needle. **Join and Decrease Row** (Right Side) K one st from front and back tog across row —

72 sts. Change to number 10 needles. K two rows.

Pattern Stitch: ROW 1 (Wrong Side) K1, P70, K1. **ROWS 2 and 4** K1, (P10, K10) three times, P10, K1. **ROWS 3 and 5** K11, (P10, K10) twice, P10, K11. **ROW 6** (Right Side) K1, *PBL 10 times, K10; repeat from * twice, PBL 10 times, K1. **ROWS 7 and 9** K1, P70, K1. **ROW 8** K across row. **ROWS 10-17** Repeat Rows 2-9. **ROWS 18-23** Repeat Rows 2-7. **ROWS 24 and 26** K11, (P10, K10) twice, P10, K11. **ROWS 25 and 27** K1, (P10, K10) three times, P10, K1. **ROW 28** (Right Side) K11, *PBL 10 times, K10; repeat from * once, PBL 10 times, K11. **ROWS 29 and 31** K1, P70, K1. **ROW 30** K across row. **ROWS 32-39** Repeat Rows 24-31. **ROWS 40-45** Repeat Rows 24-29. Repeat Rows 2-45 three times, then repeat Rows 2-23 once (piece should measure 28 inches from beginning). Bind off.

Front: Work same as for back through Increase Row of Drawstring Channel.

Drawstring Opening: ROW 1 (Right Side of Front Stitches) K across row, binding off 4 center sts in row for drawstring opening. **ROW 2** P across row, casting on 4 sts over bound-off sts of Row 1. Complete same

as for Back through Row 1 of Pattern Stitch. Begin with Row 24 of Pattern Stitch as on Back and continue in manner established through Row 45. Repeat Rows 2-45 three times, then Rows 2-29 once (piece should measure approximately 25-1/2 inches from beginning).

Divide for Neck: Next Row Continuing established pattern throughout, work across 28 sts, join another ball of yarn and bind off next 16 sts, work across remaining 28 sts. Working both sides at same time, from neck edge, bind off 3 sts once, 2 sts once and one st once — 22 sts remaining each side. Work even on both sides until front equals back to shoulder. Bind off.

Sleeves: With number 8 needles, cast on 38 sts. Work ribbing (K1, P1) for 3-1/2 inches, ending on wrong side. Change to number 10 needles. **Next Row** (Increase Row) K and inc 4 sts evenly spaced across row — 42 sts. **ROW 1** (Wrong Side) P across. **ROWS 2 and 4** P6, K10, P10, K10, P6. **ROWS 3 and 5** K6, P10, K10, P10, K6. **ROW 6** PBL six times, K10, PBL 10 times, K10, PBL six times. **ROW 7** P across row. **ROW 8** (Increase Row) K across row, inc one st each side of row — 44 sts. **ROW 9** P across row. **ROWS 10 and 12** P7, K10, P10, K10, P7.

ROWS 11 and 13 K7, P10, K10, P10, K7. **ROW 14** PBL seven times, K10, PBL 10 times, K10, PBL seven times. **ROW 15** P across row. **ROW 16** (Increase Row) Inc one st in first st, K6, P10, K10, P10, K6, inc one st in last st — 46 sts. **ROWS 17 and 19** P8, K10, P10, K10, P8. **ROW 18** K8, P10, K10, P10, K8. **ROW 20** K8, *PBL 10 times, K10, repeat from *, ending K8. Continue to work in manner established, working all row repeats until 17-1/2 inches from beginning, ending after a full row repeat has been worked with a P row, and, *at same time*, inc one st each side of row every 8th row nine more times, working new sts into pattern — 64 sts. Bind off.

Finishing: Sew shoulder seams. Mark side edges 10 inches from shoulder seams on front and back. Position bound-off edge of sleeves between markers and sew in place. Sew side and sleeve seams with care, keeping drawstring on lower body open all around.

Neck Band: With circular needles, begin at left shoulder seam and pick up 44 sts around front neck edge and 38 sts across back neck edge — 82 sts. Join and work in ribbing for 1 inch. Bind off.

Drawstring: Measure a 6-yard length of yarn, but do not cut.

76

Form a slip knot at the 6-yard point. *Do not twist or turn yarn while working.* **Step 1:** Put right index finger through lp from top, pull a lp from right yarn source through lp, hold knot with right hand, pull left yarn source and tighten. **Step 2:** Put left index finger through lp from top, pull a lp from left yarn source through lp, hold knot with left hand, pull right yarn source and tighten. Repeats Steps 1 and 2 until the drawstring is approximately 65 inches long. Fasten off. Thread through drawstring channel.

Hood: With number 8 needles, cast on 128 sts for front edge of hood. Work in ribbing for five rows. Change to number 9 needles. **Decrease Row** (Right Side) K across, dec 16 sts evenly spaced across row — 112 sts. P one row. Work in stockinette and dec one st each side of next row (neck edges) and every 4th row six times more — 98 sts. P one row.

Divide for Center Curve: K across 46 sts, sl 1, K1, psso, K1, join 2nd ball of yarn and K1, K2 tog, K remaining sts. **Note:**

Work both sides at once with separate balls of yarn through remainder of hood. **ROW 2** P across. **ROW 3** K across, dec one st at each neck edge. **ROW 4** P across row. **ROW 5** K across to within 3 sts of center curve, sl 1, K1, psso, K1 (center of hood); K1, K2 tog, K remaining sts. **ROW 6** P across row. **ROW 7** Dec one st at beginning of row, K to within 3 sts of center curve, sl 1, K1, psso, K1 (center of hood); K1, K2 tog, K to end of row, dec one st at end of row. **ROW 8** P across row. **ROW 9** Repeat Row 5. **ROW 10** P across row. **ROWS 11-20** Dec one st at each neck edge on next row and every 4th row once, and then every 2nd row twice, and, *at same time*, bind off 2 sts from center curve edge five times — 29 sts each side. Bind off. (The bound-off edge of hood is center back.) Sew the center back seam and the curved edge together. Position neck edge of hood around neck edge of sweater under neck band, easing to fit, and sew in place to pick up row of neck band.

Other Books From
The CLASSIC COLLECTION

TATTING PATTERNS $6.95

COLLARS TO KNIT AND CROCHET $6.95

AFGHANS TO CROCHET $7.95

U.S. STATE QUILT BLOCKS $6.95

**THE COMPLETE BOOK OF
JIFFY NEEDLE TATTING** $18.95

JIFFY NEEDLE TATTING, A TO Z $8.95

JIFFY NEEDLE TATTING, QUICK & EASY $8.95

**JIFFY NEEDLE TATTING,
EXCITING FASHION ACCESSORIES** $8.95

**JIFFY NEEDLE TATTING,
HOLIDAY COLLECTION** $8.95

LOVELY LACES (Large Print) $9.95

BOUTIQUE BONANZA $9.95

MORE GREAT AFGHANS $9.95